Lady SOLDIERS

AN ANTHOLOGY

Short Stories of Motivation and Survival

THE BOOK FOR ALL WOMEN

Regina E. Hudson
Chaunacey A. Hill
Janaliz Lebreault
Melanie M. Nunez
Sonia Quiles

Love yourself first

Thank You For Your Support! You Are Appreciated,

Editing: Tanisha Stewart
tanishastewart.author@gmail.com

Formatting: Iesha Bree
coversmyway@gmail.com

Cover Design: Visionary Acts
visionaryacts1@gmail.com

First Edition

Published in the United States
by Lady Soldiers

Dedication

This book is dedicated to our ancestors, to all women who are currently hurting, women who are healing, and women who are fighting every day to survive. This book stands as a reminder that

A woman's essence is like that of a rose, but her petals are made of armor!

(Artist Jillian Beth, founder of Studio Rebels in Springfield, Massachusetts creates her depiction of our camouflage rose)
The camouflage rose is our symbol for the strength and beauty of a woman.

ACKNOWLEDGMENTS

Elaine Torres, Ada Torres, Shirley Givan-Hudson, and Jessica A. Torres. As our fight continues to survive, I just need you to know that your presence in my life is irreplaceable. You are the reason I am who I am. To my son Juelz, thank you for making me stronger and accountable for our future. I hope you know that every choice I have made was to create a better life for us. To the men in my life, father, step-father, and brothers, thank you for being you. I won't stop fighting to win.-Regina

Ziyah C. Ervin, My Butterfly! Thank you for making me a mother and pushing forth my realization in understanding I am capable of all things I strive for. Mommy will continue to make you proud. To my sister my Piscean Protege Rayshandra C. Hill, thank you for always being my backbone, my number one supporter and for continuously reminding me who I am. My mother Barbara Johnson for teaching her children to be strong and resilient. To my Luvbug Hiyaz, I can't wait to make beautiful memories with you. To Rasheen, thank you for always having my back and keeping me focused. I love you all unconditionally!-Chaunacey

My late sister Jasmine and my grandmother, Magaly. My mother Iris and my younger sisters. To all the victims and survivors of domestic violence and to all the strong and beautiful women in my life and around the world.- Melanie

My children. This serves as a reminder that THERE'S A HERO THAT LIES WITHIN YOU! My mother, sisters, and everyone suffering in silence! Your job is to love you! -Janaliz

My children, Stephanie "Fany", Francisco, Diana, and Justine. As my oldest, Fany has walked this journey with me. We grew up together, facing many challenges and looking for a better opportunity in life. My son Francisco is the first man I ever loved and he showed me how to be brave enough to continue in this journey.

Diana, your unconditional support through my darkest time in life has placed you in my heart in a special way. To my baby Justine who showed me how difficult it is sometimes to be a mother, but how lovely and powerful is to hear the word "Mom" and to never give up.

Finally, I must acknowledge God who gave me the opportunity to be reborn and to transform my life by giving me the understanding that only I can control my actions and that He patiently loves me unconditionally, teaching me to love others in the same way, and He lifts me every single time.-Sonia

A woman's downfall or blooming success is based on her resilience: her ability to bounce back. To pick up the pieces. The thickness of her skin.

They say wounds and scars turn into beauty marks. Marks left on her body from battles of survival, love, and pain.

But it's not just the exterior that has to heal. A woman's interior, her mind, her heart, her soul, is the toughest to heal. The toughest to mend and put back together.

Through life's trials and tribulations, certain situations will either make or break you.

As lady soldiers, we have learned to take the punches of life. We have learned to put on body armor. We have learned that every woman, every human, has to metamorphosize and evolve. Life can seem like a battle. Casualties, triumphs, losses, wounds, allies, and enemies.

But overcoming the battle is the most rewarding part.

The biggest battle comes from within. The biggest battle comes from overcoming fear, overcoming obstacles, and using your armor as protection to no longer be hurt or wounded by anyone or anything.

The biggest battle is understanding that as women, we are stronger together. Every woman is a survivor. Every woman is a queen. Every woman is a soldier.

Regina

"Be thankful for your guardian angel. Whoever it is, wherever they are, believe it or not - they are protecting you. They are keeping you alive for a reason. Find that reason. Find your purpose." -Regina Hudson

Introduction

She was that book smart, clumsy, acne-faced, insecure young girl.

She now is that woman who looks at a challenge and approaches it with no fear. She has blossomed with confidence and faith. She is strong. SHE IS ME.

1

. . .

DISPLACED SHOULDER. I could see my shoulder bone abnormally risen and popped out of place, deformed from being slammed to the floor, fighting my ex.

Bruises on my neck from being choked, gasping for air, gasping to be loved.

Police lights outside, flashlights shown through my window.

As a new mother I ended up single, broken, embarrassed, and betrayed.

That 1:30 a.m. phone call is what changed it all.

Sad to say but many of us women know that infidelity is too common. Giving ourselves to men who do not deserve us; too common.

I got up from the bed since he had fallen asleep on the couch watching TV. I began poking him in his head.

As he woke up, I screamed, *"Who the F is ...".*

He was stunned and he reached for his phone in my hand.

War began.

I remember being on the floor trying to block my face. Looking in the mirror at my displaced shoulder trying to pop it back into place. Looking at my broken household, knowing that it was my responsibility to put the pieces back together. As a woman, it always seems to be my responsibility to hold it all together, for myself and others at times.

As a new mother I ended up single, broken, embarrassed, and betrayed with a side of social services watching us to make sure my home "was safe" for my son. Single motherhood, toxic relationships, and domestic violence is nothing pretty.

IGNORING THE RED FLAGS COULD COST YOU IT ALL.

Flashback

Flashbacking to my childhood.

Some things I remember so vividly.

I was blessed with a two-parent household, a mom and step-dad. Step-dad was superman, mom was strong. Being blessed always has its curses attached. I always felt displaced like I didn't belong. I had the darkest skin in my household. Five times darker than my household, hair ten times thicker. I felt like the odd ball. I struggled with myself, with accepting myself. Only saw and criticized my physical. When you're young, it's hard to understand self-love and that everyone has insecurities; that the outside appearance is insignificant to one's true self.

I was that girl who was clumsy, yet book smart. I was 4'11, very curvy, very mature, suffered with acne, suffered with a bad attitude a.k.a. insecure, *suffered with the I Don't Know Who I am or Don't Like Who I Am Syndrome.* It followed me for years. I couldn't break that insecure mindset. I felt ugly. I was called ugly. My confidence was lower than low.

As I write this, I need you to know that *self discovery and self acceptance are key.*

Do what you have to do to love yourself, whether it's removing those toxic people, having walks in the park, exercising, reading, writing, therapy, quitting your job, or connecting with other women.

Do it all, because that's exactly what I've done to begin to find my peace.

Lost

Since adolescence, the *I don't know who I am or like who I am syndrome* took me to dark places, low points, ambulance rides, bruises, fat lips, and single motherhood.

But on the bright side, I am thankful for my guardian angel.

If it wasn't for my guardian angel I have no idea where I would have ended up, but I don't think it would have been anywhere good or alive.

The blackouts are when it really got bad.

Binge drink until you black out, drink until you forget, drink to fit in.

That self monitoring, knowing your limit will do you some favors.

I found peace.

That's what I thought it was in blunts, liquor, music, men, and working.

As I made it through college by the skin of my teeth, the darkness still lived. It followed me. I never realized that healing and self-love takes time, new activities, positive activities, and practice. Self-love takes *discipline and reflection*.

How many times do we experience something painful and

just "move on". Keep pushing, keep trying to survive. What is the proper way to handle the aftermath? What is the proper way to make sure that that experience does not hinder us?

I found myself in many toxic relationships with men. I lived in the delusional and fantasy world. *What I did wrong was love others more than myself.*

I always wondered the effects my DNA had on me.

Do you believe in generational effects or curses?

I definitely do but I also believe that those curses can be broken with commitment and self-reflection. Mom was super-woman but tired; father and uncles are loyal to narcotics anonymous as previous addicts; alcoholism runs deep; there has been single motherhood and domestic violence in every generation; and grandad died in prison.

The curse of addiction, depression, loving hard, and stubbornness was in my blood.

It's taken all of me to recognize this and put this in a book, turn it into positivity.

Turning your lessons into positivity and believing in yourself is when you truly start living.

Single Mom Strong

I remember these specific text messages.

The text messages from someone who I had given years of my life to.

"I Hope You Die", B***ch I Hate You, You Ain't Nothing But a Who*e".

It still blows my mind to this day. Not one thing about this is healthy, and I am glad I finally was able to walk away.

Single motherhood has been one of my toughest battles because it takes a mental toll, daily. Am I a failure because I'm not with the father? Does my son know that I am trying my best? These questions run through my mind constantly. When you sleep alone, when you raise a child alone, when you wake up for another day with just you and your baby, mentally it takes a toll.

Battles of child support, financial and his actual presence is another piece of this lifestyle. Do I fight for support or just let it go? Will I be alone for the rest of my life? Will my son be happy?

That point in our insecure lives when we feel comfortable being in a toxic relationship is when things go downhill, fast.

Comfortable just being in any kind of a relationship, as long as we are in one.

My son must have been about three-months-old.

He had digestive problems with his formula, which caused many doctor visits and formula changes. At home one night like many others, he was crying because of his stomach. I tried soothing him, rocking him, but he would not fall asleep.

As I stood in the kitchen holding him, rocking him, do you know what projectile vomit means? At that very moment I found out. Within two seconds (I swear it was like an exorcism, as his mouth jolted open) I was covered in vomit.

My hair, the side of my face, my shoulder, and all over him.

I remember screaming.

Of course I was home alone.

Time to clean up baby and I. Oh, the amount of times I have cleaned up vomit and diarrhea alone. I might have done this more than I can count by now, cleaning it from my car, the tub, the floor, my body; you name it, I probably cleaned it.

That is motherhood.

I went back to work after only five weeks of the C section maternity leave.

We needed money.

One time I was getting ready for work and he was a few months old. I gathered my items together: purse, lunch, baby, baby bag.

As I lugged things to the car, I placed the baby bag on the front step. Rushed to the car, packed it all up. Pulled off, drove to grandma's, dropped off my son, headed to work.

Then the lightbulb goes off - I left the baby bag on the stairs.

Called work crying, saying I was going to be late. Back to home I go.

Trips to the ER, multiple trips to the doctors, sleepless nights.

That is motherhood.

On the other hand, motherhood is unconditional love, hugs

and kisses, and a strength you didn't know existed. The struggle of a working mother, it never ends, and *it doesn't get easier, but it can get better.*

Sometimes as a single mother, you truly get scared.

Scared not knowing what is to come. Scared because you wonder if you and your child will make it through. Scared that what if one day you feel like you can't do it anymore, that you give up. Scared wondering if your child will be happy, will be healthy in every way.

Another diagnosis I see in many single mothers, I call it the *single mom syndrome*: depressed, unmotivated, lonely, broken, crying out for love, yet still showing up for another day to make sure their children are taken care of. I am pushing myself to defeat these common traits.

I know that I can't let single motherhood defeat me or hinder my progress.

Giving up can never be an option. My son's life depends on me.

Freedom

All at once, from leaving that relationship, to withdrawing all my savings and other means to purchase a home, to the surprise of terrible tenants and evicting them, to struggling in my career, to starting my own business, to forcing ends to meet financially where I had to pawn jewelry, count change, and strategize to pay bills, to questioning my abilities and future, the last few years almost caused a hospital admittance.

Yet what still drives me is life itself, opportunity.

Opportunity to grow and become who I am supposed to be.

Opportunity to tell my story in hopes that another woman won't feel alone, and/or maybe won't put herself in the same situations I have.

So I took the opportunity to book myself a vacation (Splurge!). And that was the best decision I could have made. For someone who had just gotten out of a six year relationship, I lived, ate, and breathed my partner and motherhood for every second while in that relationship. For those six years I never went on a vacation for me, I wasn't living for me. It was time to let go and see what life had to offer. Jamaica was everything I thought it would be: beautiful, fun, welcoming people. Palm trees, reggae, and of course rum punch.

Five days I had the pleasure. Five days I was around people who worked their behinds off for little money because we ignore it, but other countries aren't as fortunate financially as the U.S.

For five days I was around people who loved music and fun in a space where I felt free. This was the best gift I could have given myself.

Taking a break is very necessary, a weekend away, a week away - give yourself time to regroup and breathe.

Healing & Growing

The past few years broke me down to the core - but the past few years also showed me how resilient I am, and how life can be rebuilt.

Everything happens for a reason; cause and effect. When we look back and see how things played out, see how things manifested, we realize that a good portion of our lives we have created. We refuse to acknowledge this sometimes. We tend to forget how we got where we are. We tend to not want to take responsibility for our actions and decisions.

I realized that my broken or misunderstood spirit wanted to love and care for others who were broken just like me. I also realized that my insecure mind caused me to put myself into situations I never should have been in!

Interestingly enough, I have used my pain and lessons learned to push me forward. I've become involved within my community. I speak at different events on entrepreneurship and financial literacy. I host events for women empowerment and networking. I encourage people to step out of their comfort zone. I surround myself with positive people, positive women. I force myself to attend positive events, networking, and community oriented. I encourage people to do what I've done and pursue their dreams and passions.

Healing and growth is imperative. Imperative for a better future. But many times because of emotion and irrational thinking we move forward without healing, without processing a painful situation. Just on to the next. After a few years of rebuilding, I am continuing to move forward wiser, stronger, and hopeful. *As I continue to heal – I hope that you will heal with me.*

"I like to play a strong woman but a strong woman can also be very fragile and vulnerable at the same time."
-Carice Von Houten

Artist: TMP of Springfield, MA draws a woman as he interprets, carrying the world on her back.

Your Greatest Weapon

Your greatest weapon starts from within
You are your greatest weapon
Your hope, your ambition, your confidence
Believing in yourself is key
The inability to feel threatened
The ability to protect yourself
The understanding of yourself
The ability to see that you have purpose
The ability to know that yes you are worth it
Do not forfeit, do not throw in the towel
Because you are your greatest weapon.
-Regina E. Hudson

Stages of Emotional Healing

1. *Awareness - Emotional awareness is imperative. It is imperative to accept and grow through your trauma. Recognizing how you are feeling and why will later invite you to a healthier way of living. To become aware, you need to mentally re-live what happened. Identify the root of the problem and identify if there is anything you should have done differently. LEARN FROM THE SITUATION.*
2. *Expression - You need to validate and release your feelings. Whether you have to cry, shake, yell, journal, walk, exercise - find something soothing and do it daily to regulate your emotions. It is also highly recommended to talk to someone about what you have experienced, whether it be a friend or therapist, or both. Make sure you talk to someone.*
3. *Reflection - Self-reflection helps us to take control and create new positive meaning. Self-reflection will give you the opportunity to create new inspiration, meaning, and purpose.*
4. *Transformation - Transform the negative emotions into positive ones. This can be done through the use of a daily gratitude or appreciation practice. Positive self-talk and experiences will*

provide a foundation for you to build the life and woman you were meant to be.

Chaunacey

"Life is your canvas; paint it as you please."
~Chaunie Crafts~

<u>THE BUTTERFLY</u>

These butterflies in my stomach have been fluttering for three days now. I'm not nervous about anything. I mean the rent is due as usual, but my grandmother always told me to "let go and let God". I can't take this strange feeling anymore. Why is it consistent? I tell my fiancé and he jokingly says, "Maybe you're pregnant?"

Pregnant! When, where, how? Well I know how but ...Florida. It had to have been our vacation in Florida. I had the time of my life. The beaches were beautiful, the palm trees were... wait!

Am I pregnant?

I rushed to my local drug store and purchased three pregnancy tests. Lord only knows why I purchased three. After reading the instructions I came to the conclusion that it would be best to take them in the morning. Apparently that's when urine is the most potent. That night was the longest night of my life.

The next morning I sat on the toilet anxious, scared, and worried, but peeking at me through the bathroom door was my fiancé. I'm sure his face looked more concerned than mine.

We made eye contact and began chuckling together. I was so in love with this man and in that moment all of my anxiety went away.

He barged through the door, reached over me and grabbed one of the soaked pregnancy tests off of the sink. He looked down at it and then back up at me and said nothing. He then reached over and grabbed the other two.

"Well!" I said desperately, awaiting his response.

After what seemed like the world's longest pause he said, "The flutters must be from the Butterfly you're carrying."

"Carrying," I said frantically.

"Yes; you're carrying our Butterfly." I've never seen his smile so big.

I was speechless. I couldn't move. I sat on the toilet for so long my legs went numb. So many thoughts went through my mind. *Am I ready to be a mom? Can I afford to be a mother?* Tears began to form. I was terrified. I placed my face in my hands as if I was hiding from reality.

The man I loved so dearly removed them from my face, lifted me off the toilet, looked me in my eyes and said, "We're going to be okay. You'll be the best mother in the world. I know it with every part of my being."

I knew in this moment my life would change but never could I be prepared for what was to come.

The Cocoon

Things have been so hard lately.

My body aches, food tastes strange and even when it doesn't it comes right up.

I've been praying to the porcelain Gods a lot lately and work - phew, that's another story.

I had to reflect on why I'm even going to that place. I mean it is a humbling position. To assist adults with mental health delays gave me a sense of purpose for a long time.

Whenever I thought life was rough my arrival to that facility was a clear reminder that I am truly blessed to even have the simple things that so many people took for granted, myself included. Yet while pregnant I felt I needed just as much attention as my clients, if not more.

Furthermore, I just couldn't grasp why women are required to work while pregnant. Especially after six years of employment with the same company.

Day in and day out I would stress myself with thoughts like, *How am I going to manage paying on this rent while on maternity leave? Will the lights get shut off? How can I find my crying daughter with no damn lights?*

Candle light dinners I enjoy, but a candle light life? No. I'm all set with that.

The days seemed so much longer now but when my Butterfly fluttered, all those stressful thoughts went out the window. Wow, I was going to bring a little girl into this world. I was going to be a mommy.

After work one day, I rushed home.

The red lights seemed to stay red longer than usual. I convinced myself the government had everything to do with it. I was so anxious to get home to the man I loved. My strong, sexy, loc-headed black man. I just knew there was a war on black men and the government was trying to keep me away from him. I know there is a war on the black family. I began to have visions of Marcus Garvey driving a tank, demolishing the traffic lights yelling, "Yesssss get to your King, Goddess!"

Okay. Okay. Maybe I was delusional.

When I arrived home I ran up the stairs so fast. It may have been a slight jog, but whatever.

I got to the door so anxious to kiss the man I loved so dearly, the man that was going to help me raise the best human being in the world.

Finally, I got the key in the door and there he was sitting on the couch, staring at the wall.

I said... nothing.

Instead I dashed off to the bathroom.

Nausea was my newfound best friend and the toilet is where I spent most of my life these days. After what seemed like an eternity of releasing the nothing that was in my stomach, I brushed my teeth and headed to the living room with the biggest smile on my face. So anxious to kiss the lips of my King.

He was sitting in the same spot still staring into space.

I knew something was wrong. I sat next to him.

He looked me in the eyes with a blank stare and his lips never moved.

"My love, what's wrong?" I asked. "Please don't tell me you're worried about our Butterfly. I've been doing a lot of thinking lately and we-"

He interjected, "Granny has cancer. Stage four cancer."

"Wait what?" I said with the feeling of my heart dropping to my stomach.

Granny was his everything. He loved her so much. She was the rock in his family.

I was speechless. This was supposed to be the happiest time of our lives but here we were, wrapped in each other's arms, faces flooded with tears, souls saturated with sorrow.

Then, she kicked.

Road Trip

Getting to granny was detrimental.

This was a case of drop everything and run.

The road trip seemed to take forever and it was as if my bladder was worse on the road.

Every 10 minutes I required a toilet and a snack. I knew my love was anxious but he kept his composure the whole time.

Five hours later, we finally reached the Bronx.

New York always had a smell of ocean, garbage, and love. The scent hit me like a ton of bricks when I stepped out of the car. Usually that was warm and inviting but with this baby baking in me I was appalled. It was as if I was standing in the middle of the worlds' largest landfill while standing next to a man devouring a sauerkraut-filled Coney Island dog.

I instantly became nauseous. Perhaps our Butterfly was no fan of New York.

It was a marathon getting to the 5th floor. I never realized how much of a task it was.

Finally, there before us was Granny's door. I swear I glistened like a Christmas tree. Fear, worry and sadness took over my body.

My love grabbed my hand and led the way. We were greeted by his aunt and made our way to the living room.

There she laid. It was as if the bed swallowed her fragile body. She was so tiny. She appeared so fragile. As we got closer to her, she opened her eyes and said, "Hey babies".

In that moment her spirit filled the room; it was indeed larger than life.

Granny had this warmth about her. She had the ability to pull every ounce of love out of you. It was impossible to speak to her without having a smile on your face and love in your eyes. I absolutely adored this woman and although she was my fiancé's grandmother, she never treated me like anything less than her own.

WE LAID in bed with Granny for hours. We talked about memories, her delicious meals and how my love was hard headed growing up but still could always seek refuge with Granny.

She was excited about our Butterfly. She continually looked at my belly and asked if I was okay. I could see the love in her eyes for our unborn child already and in that moment I knew our Butterfly would carry her namesake. I was excited about it.

There was one thing that excited Granny more than our Butterfly, more than her favorite grandsons' arrival, more than seeing the family and that was that Barack Obama was the first black president to grace the White House alongside a beautiful black woman and two daughters. She had lived to see it. She was so proud.

OUR WHOLE STAY was filled with love. We didn't want to leave her. If I could have kidnapped Granny and brought her home I would have. It wasn't until the car ride home that we realized she was indeed very fragile and extremely sick. Our days with Granny were numbered and we knew it.

The ride home was silent. I constantly looked over at my love and saw the tears in his eyes. He was doing his best to keep it together for me.

My tears were uncontrollable. My head throbbed. My face

was sore from the constriction of crying. How long did Granny have? Could the doctors have been wrong about her diagnosis? Would she live to see our Butterfly born? So many thoughts and emotions filled my body.

Then, she kicked.

Nursery and the Nonsense

WEEKS later the nausea began to ease up.

My energy began to return. I even took on a second job.

My whole mind state was to save as much money as we could. As far as I was concerned, my daughter needed a college fund and I needed to begin saving as soon as possible.

Not to mention, her arrival date was about two months away.

We began to decorate her room. We went with the idea of a flower garden. What better theme for a butterfly? The room was coming together. The large mural was almost complete. My hand-crafted flowers hung in each corner. I was so proud of the space we created for her. I just knew she'd love it.

Then there was my favorite corner.

There I envisioned spending summer nights rocking back and forth singing some of my favorite songs to my Butterfly until she fell asleep. I couldn't wait for our new life journey.

As the days went on everyone became more excited for our Butterfly's arrival.

As for myself, I became a robot. Work, home, work on the nursery, make dinner, head back to work, return home, work on the nursery, go to bed, wake up and do it all again.

I swore nothing was perfect enough.

I did not understand this new clean freak energy that came over me. It was so bad my fiancé literally removed a toothbrush from my hands because I was on my hands and knees scrubbing invisible dirt, if you ask him.

For me the dirt was there and magnified. I couldn't understand how we lived in such filth for so long. To be honest I just may have been overdoing it but I didn't care.

Our Butterfly deserved to come home to a squeaky clean environment.

I was on a quest to give her heaven on earth.

The Loss

THE TIME HAD COME to visit Granny.

Now seven months pregnant, I was unable to take the trip. My back would ache, my feet were swollen, and I had no patience for a long car ride so I stayed behind.

My love promised to give me a call when he and his children arrived so I could speak with her. While home, I prepped flowers for our upcoming baby shower. I wrote out lists of items needed and prepped the menu. None of this was my job but I wanted perfection.

In those moments you would have thought my expertise was party planning.

That day I created a large tree on the wall, added appliqués to each corner then there I stood in front of the window, wondering whether to put up pink or purple curtains.

The phone rang.

"Hey my love," I said.

There was no response.

"Bae, hello, are you there?"

He said in the most somber tone, "She's gone."

"Oh no!"

He told me he and the children walked into the house and found Granny in bed unresponsive. That was the last time I stepped foot in that nursery.

It died when Granny did. My better half would never be the

same and I knew there was nothing I could do to change it. How could I do this without the strength of my King?

Farewell

THE FUNERAL WAS UNBEARABLE.

I hated to see my fiancé with so much pain in his eyes and I felt selfish even bringing up our Butterfly. How could I when our family and friends were mourning the loss of an amazing woman?

That day the cramps I had were extremely uncomfortable.

I couldn't enjoy the service. I spent the majority of the time in the bathroom trying to hide my pain from others then ultimately spent the rest of the time trying to get comfortable and resting in the car. I didn't want to stay inside in that condition.

Didn't want Granny's going home service to be about me.

This was supposed to be a happy time.

Granny was supposed to meet her namesake.

The depression set in, and then she kicked.

I Could Never Imagine

TWO WEEKS later my midwife appointment arrived.

I battled terrible heartburn the night before and couldn't wait to speak with the nurses and other mothers in my birthing group about it. I was told an old myth that heartburn while pregnant was an indication that your child was going to have a full head of hair.

Based off of the heartburn I had the night before, I just knew I'd be giving birth to Rapunzel.

My midwife appointments consisted of a urine sample, a

blood pressure test, and my favorite part: hearing your baby's heartbeat.

I laid down so excited to hear the beat from my Butterfly.

I waited patiently, but nothing.

I looked at the nurse and by her face I could instantly tell something was wrong.

"What's going on?" I asked.

She stated that something may be wrong with her machine and for me to head to the back to see another nurse. Once in the back, the results were the same - no heartbeat.

I was then advised to make my way to the Emergency Room.

I couldn't breathe. What was going on? Where was my Butterfly's heartbeat?

Perhaps both machines were faulty.

I called my fiance.

He said he'd meet me at the hospital.

I then called my best friend. She had a way of keeping me level headed and I needed that in this moment.

She too was on her way.

Once he arrived, I had a small sense of relief at seeing my love's face.

We were brought to a dark room and waited for an ultrasound. There she appeared on the screen, just as beautiful as ever.

I thought about how it would feel to hold her in my arms. I couldn't wait to smell her. Would she look more like me or her father? Would she have brown eyes and brown hair?

I wondered what profession she'd choose then I heard the words that will replay in my mind until my last day on Earth.

"I'M SORRY. YOUR DAUGHTER IS NO LONGER LIVING."

I grew silent.

I couldn't comprehend.

How? What? When?

None of this made sense.

I began to cry uncontrollably and in that moment I met the true feeling of heartbreak. My first born. Our future, our legacy, my everything, she was gone, and I could do nothing about it.

My love's face was filled with devastation.

We held each other and cried for what seemed like eternity.

Have I failed as a woman? What was wrong with me? I knew so many unfit mothers. Why did I not even get the chance to try?

Where is God? What God? He couldn't exist. If he was a loving God then why did he hate me? I was brought into a room where I was prepped for labor and delivery.

Never could I imagine I'd be a woman who'd birth death.

A Mother of Death

I felt as if I was in a simulated game in that delivery room.

This is where I'd meet my Butterfly.

This is where her father would cut her umbilical cord.

This is where I'd hear her first cry, but she wouldn't be crying at all. In fact I'd never hear her cry. I'd never get to sing to her in my favorite corner rocking in my favorite chair.

I cried even more.

I was told I had a severe case of preeclampsia with a rare condition called HELLP Syndrome.

I was lucky to be alive.

Lucky!

How could this doctor tell a woman who is preparing to birth death anything about being lucky? In the blink of an eye I went from up and alert to dizzy and exhausted. I knew something was wrong.

I felt as if my spirit was leaving my body.

My memory is blurry from this point but I do recall the doctor telling me I may not make it through this.

I was rushed into surgery for an emergency C section.

I woke to the most beautiful sight I'd ever seen.

The nurse approached me holding my swaddled Butterfly.

She was perfect.

I saw so many faces in hers. My grandmother, mother, her father, his mother, myself.

This feeling of love was nothing I'd ever felt in my 28 years of life. I adored and inspected every part of her tiny body. I began to remove her onesie. I couldn't wait to see her neck, her arms, her everything.

Those feelings were quickly changed when I met the plastic her body was wrapped with.

This was done in order to keep her skin from falling off.

It was then that I recognized the blood running from her nose.

Reality then set in.

She was dead...DEAD!

The time came for me to say my goodbyes.

Just like a Butterfly, she graced me with her beauty then flew away, all in an instant.

It was that day that I became the mother of a Butterfly.

The Metamorphosis

LIFE WAS NO LONGER where I wanted it to be.

The pain in my body was nothing compared to the pain of loss. The milk from my breasts leaked constantly. I cried every day. I visited every emotion a human could experience.

I became selfish and extremely introverted as if I was the last person on Earth.

My relationship began to fail and I felt I failed him.

After much deliberation I finally figured things out.

I could never just take my life... but what if my life was taken?

<u>One year later</u>

MY BUTTERFLY'S anniversary arrived and unbeknownst to anyone, I had a death wish. I woke up early that morning, life insurance papers prepped in my glove box, along with a will stating that my sister gets everything!

I took a drive to the rural area of Orange, Massachusetts to face my fate and I was excited about it. When pulling in the parking lot, I could see colorful balloon lookalikes falling from the sky. I watched as they descended. Their silhouettes morphing from tiny figures to people.

Watching everyone land was exhilarating and I was there to be one of those people.

The instructive class seemed to take forever. The whole conversation was a blur.

I was just ready to jump and soar, just like my Butterfly.

Things didn't really begin to settle in until I was actually getting suited up.

My instructor prepped meticulously to make sure our jump would be safe and the parachute would deploy.

Little did he know I was prepared to die that day.

During the plane ride, memories went through my mind. *Was this going to be it for me? I don't want to survive but what if I do?* My second time on a plane and I'm jumping out of it - what would my mom say? So many thoughts flooded my brain.

They came to a halt when I heard the videographer say, "Hey Chaunie, look out the window. How are you feeling?"

I looked out.

The birds' eye view was beautiful.

I told him I was excited.

He said, "Well we're now at 1500 feet. We'll be jumping at 18000 feet. See you soon."

My Wings

THE DOORS of the plane opened.

This was it. The moment I'd face destiny.

My instructor and I scooted down to the doors. The sky was very different from my regular view. Filled with puffy white clouds. I could reach out and touch them. Here I was sitting at the edge of the door, feet tucked under the plane, arms crossed, with not one ounce of fear in my body. Worst-case scenario, I'd meet death but I wanted to.

Death is where my daughter was and she needed me.

How could I fear death when I gave birth to it?

Then we jumped!!!

The initial fall was extreme. It felt just as it did in my dreams.

That feeling only lasted a few seconds. In an instant we were floating, supported by the sky.

I spread my wings and flew, just like my Butterfly!

When my feet finally touched the ground I realized I was here for a reason.

It was that moment I innerstood that my Butterfly sacrificed her wings for me and she didn't leave me at all.

In fact, she was my gift of life packaged as death.

From that moment forward I vowed to make her proud of me. I was and am forever a mother. A mother of an Angel. The mother of a Butterfly.

I chose life!

A Metamorphosis Continues

THEY SAY death comes in threes.

Six months later I buried my father.

Although that was yet another painful time, my Butterfly taught me not to hate death nor fear it. Granny, my daughter, and my father all in the course of nine months. Frankly, how could I hate or fear death when it is something that I birthed?

Death was now part of me and I now strived to put death to things in my life that didn't serve me or make me happy. I went most of my life caring about what others thought of me. I had a quest for perfection that I'd never be able to uphold.

These days I lived to make my Butterfly proud and didn't care how anyone else felt about it. I took the time to do "womb work" to go within and fall in love with myself.

I now had purpose.

With that attitude, I pushed my artistic capabilities to a new level. I instructed numerous art classes, produced and hosted an online radio show, graced stages as a featured musical artist and made the local paper a few times.

My paintings and cakes were selling, commissioned work was continuous and much more.

I was even cast in a college musical.

Did I mention I never went to college?

This was all thanks to my Butterfly.

I used the pain as motivation. Metamorphosis is never easy; it is extremely painful but very much necessary.

My Butterfly sacrificed her wings in order for me to fly and for her generous and selfless choice I evolved from Chaunacey to what I ran from for years. I now embrace the creative energy that flows through me. **I am Chaunie Crafts!**

An Earthly Goodbye

THREE YEARS LATER, life was good.

So much so that my fiance and I got back together. We were

told this would be impossible after such a tragedy and although we went through hardships, in the end, love took the victory.

The time came for us to release the remains of our Butterfly.

It felt right. She had to be released from her urn. An urn was no place for a Butterfly.

Her father and I booked a trip to Florida, back to where she was created and released her remains into the ocean so she'd be able to travel the world.

This was such an emotional day but these were different tears.

Tears of relief, tears of joy, tears of growth and unconditional love.

A Butterflies return

HEADING BACK TO OUR HOTEL, there was this weight that had been lifted from us.

It felt promising, like we had completed a mission for our soul.

Once we reached the elevator I was abruptly reminded of the random nausea spells I'd been facing lately.

Inside my spirit I knew the reasoning.

I just awaited the confirmation and I'd receive it today. The results were just as I expected.

I ran out the bathroom quickly and shared the news with my love screaming at the top of my lungs......

"Sometimes in tragedy we find our life's purpose." -Robert Brault

Artist: ChaunieCrafts of Springfield Massachusetts draws an image of receiving her wings, and in turn, releasing her baby girl back to the heavens.

Joy!

Is what I had when I felt that first kick
Couldn't believe the news,
I was going to bear my first kid.
Mixed feelings, cuz I wasn't expecting it
But giving her the world is where my thought process went.
Picked up another job I'm thinking future go harder
Exhausted days on end but anything for my daughter
Fast forward 8 months another check-up as usual
Anxious to hear her heartbeat, dying to see her visuals.
Instead I'm so confused cuz they rushed me to the hospital
Ultrasound hook up, they couldn't find her blood flow, No
They didn't find her blood flow
ULTRASOUND HOOKED UP THEY NEVER FOUND HER
BLOOD FLOW!
AND I COULDN'T COMPREHEND
JUST WHAT WENT WRONG
THEY SAID PRE-ECLAMPSIA
TOPPED WITH HELLP SYNDROME
TOLD ME ANOTHER DAY
I WOULD HAVE BEEN 6 FT DEEP
SO I QUESTION GOD DAILY WHY YOU NOT ME?
I went from expecting mother
to having a daughter deceased
You know the feeling of telling a new born to rest in peace?
I told my baby girl, rest in peace.
Y'ALL KNOW THE FEELING TELLING A NEWBORN TO REST
IN PEACE?
Now I'm day to day wondering what she would have been
It's hard looking at her father cuz she looked like him.
God made the decision without me
To let your soul fly free

Now I'm stuck here releasing A capella no beat.

They say Chaunie stay strong
You gotta live on
But it's hard to live on
When your mind's so gone.
They say Chaunie be strong
You gotta live on
But it's hard to live on
When your minds so gone
DAMN!!
~Chaunie Crafts

There isn't a night that goes by that I don't dream
    of you.
I can't help but question God why would he
    separate us two.
Yes my life was on the line, I guess I'm happy to
    see another day.
But life without you,
I would have chose death anyway.
To give you life, a breath, a soul, a chance
I want to live in that moment I held you,
Reality proves I can't.
I touch my belly looking for you,
then I feel our separation scar.
I still wait to feel kicks, I want to hear your heart.
In these moments I smile, it's then washed away
    with tears.
My first child, my baby, my daughter, my dear.
You were PERFECTION,
In such an ugly world.
Your ten fingers, ten toes, two eyes, two ears, one
    mouth, one nose.
You are the best thing that's ever happened to me.
Now I have no choice but to use this pain as fuel
    to continue to chase my destiny.

Zihya!
Mommy Loves you ❤

Healing of the Womb

After the loss of my daughter I searched for answers. Answers from God, answers from doctors, then I realized the right thing to do was to go within and gain answers from myself.
You see, not practicing self-love is something that is detrimental. It literally radiates. I began to understand that everything around me was what I allowed and what I created for myself.
On my journey of healing, a cousin of mine Rainelle X introduced me to Queen Afua.
She gave me a book called the "Sacred Woman" and my life changed forever. I learned about healing of the womb and my direct connection to it. I learned about the connection between my womb and society as a whole. I recommend this book to all women and suggest even passing it onto your daughters so they too can understand the power they hold. The doctors told me my chances of having another stillbirth were very high.
They suggested I never try again.
My spirit had other plans.
I began to do the work Queen Afua suggested for me.
I changed my diet, I meditated, I did Yoni steams, I burned sage, I spoke to

my inner child, I listened to my womb and understood its trauma, I faced my
fears head on and understood life obstacles were learning experiences.
I BEGAN TO LOVE ME, WHOLE HEARTEDLY.
Now here I am carrying yet another beautiful baby girl.
WE ARE THE MOST POWERFUL BEINGS ON THIS EARTH
SIMPLY BECAUSE WE BRING FORTH LIFE. DESPITE WHAT
WAS TAUGHT TO US, THIS IS AND WILL FOREVER BE A
WOMAN'S WORLD!

"A NATION CAN RISE ONLY AS HIGH AS ITS WOMEN." -Louis
Farrakhan

"THE CONDITION OF A WOMAN'S WOMB ALSO REFLECTS
THE CONDITION OF A WOMAN'S MIND, SPIRIT, AND
ACTIONS. THE WOMB IS A STOREHOUSE OF ALL OUR
EMOTIONS. IT COLLECTS EVERY FEELING, GOOD
AND BAD.
TODAY WE HAVE COLLECTIVELY REACHED A STATE OF
"NEGATIVE WOMB POWER." UNNATURAL LIVING AND
UNHEALTHY LIFESTYLES PERPETUATE NEGATIVE WOMB
POWER, AND THIS IN TURN SUPPORTS THE CONFLICT OF
HUMANS AGAINST THE PLANET, HUMANS AGAINST
HUMANS AND WOMEN AGAINST THE WOMB.
THE CONDITION OF A WOMAN'S WOMB ALSO REFLECTS
THE CONDITION OF ALL HER RELATIONSHIPS. WHEN A
WOMAN'S WOMB IS IN A HEALTHY STATE, HER LIFE IS A
REFLECTION OF THIS BALANCE." -Queen Afua
(Sacred Woman: A Guide to Healing the Feminine Body, Mind and Spirit)

Melanie

"She lives through me." -Melanie Nunez

My Sister's Keeper

The clock on the nightstand read 3:45 a.m.

I had only been asleep for forty-five minutes but I didn't feel tired. I lay in the dark beside my mother, who hadn't stopped crying all night. I held on to her as tight as I could. I didn't know if this would help her but it helped me.

I could hear my father's footsteps pacing back and forth in the next room, at times crying out in disbelief. I wanted to hold him. I wanted to tell my parents that everything would be okay, that a miracle had occurred and my sister would be home soon, but how could I lie to them?

Everything wouldn't be okay.

Jasmine was gone.

That day we spent our morning at a Bronx Police Station in New York.

Law enforcement had worked straight through the night trying to obtain as much information as they could about my twenty-two-year-old sister, Jasmine, who we had reported missing the day before. Family, friends, and reporters had gathered outside the precinct waiting on any news of the beautiful college girl, whose radiant smile had captured the hearts of the community. Flyers were circulating through social networks and local establishments.

The news had got out and leads were coming in of possible sightings. Meanwhile, inside the police station a new lead had come in. An unidentified body of a young woman fitting my sisters' description had been found at James Baird Park in Poughkeepsie, NY.

A first generation student and the oldest of seven in a large blended Dominican family, Jasmine understood how important her role as a big sister was to her siblings. To us, she was ahead of her time. A natural born leader, confident in her purpose and yet, undeniably humble. Intelligently smooth with her words; a poet if you will. A social butterfly but surprisingly selective with whom she'd befriend and that made it easy for anyone who knew her to understand that her aura was different. A great listener, she confirmed the importance of spoken words and in the darkest of times could help you realize just how much meaning life really had. A funny, sassy and gentle soul. I don't believe there are enough words in the dictionary that could fully describe the unique being she was. Her beauty was just a plus to all the qualities she carried on the inside.

Growing up, I wanted to borrow every outfit, listen to all her

CD's and be everywhere she was. She set every trend I followed, and she loved it. Jasmine was my best friend. We spoke every day. We were inseparable. I was only two years younger than her. She loved me, she said I was her baby and would joke that she birthed me herself.

Jasmine was my only fully biological sister, which means we shared both my dad's smile and my mom's eyes. We were born in Brooklyn but relocated to Springfield, Massachusetts with my mom in 2005.

After graduating high school, Jasmine decided to return back to New York City, our roots, to further her education. She enrolled in the surgical technician program at Mandl College and was extremely excited to be returning back to school. She couldn't wait for this next chapter in her young adult life. She was just getting started.

Detectives brought my father into a room to identify my sister. We learned her body had been badly burned after she died, but it was her. It was really her.

I opened my mouth to scream but nothing would come out. My mind was racing and I felt light headed. I was confused. Nothing made sense. How could the man that we treated like family, whom we had let into our home and who said he loved my sister, murder her and then dispose of her body on the side of the road like she meant nothing? My faith and all I believed in disappeared in an instant.

I looked up just in time to see my mom's eyes roll back and her legs give out as she collapsed on the floor of the police station. Life as we knew it, was gone.

June 5th, 2011 was the last time I heard her voice. We spoke for a few hours and she told me how busy her schedule was going to be. She would be working and attending classes full time. As our conversation came to an end, I told her how proud I was of her and that I loved her. I knew that was all she ever wanted, the confirmation from her family that she was on the right path and making us proud.

After taking Jasmine's life, he killed himself.

We received no answers.

Just a timeline of events that spread over a two week period.

A bunch of puzzle pieces that didn't fit.

Why? Where? When?

No answers.

The detectives kept throwing around this term, Domestic Violence.

No, they were wrong. Jasmine was the opposite of everything society told us *battered women* were: timid, co-dependent, isolated, depressed. How ignorant and naive of me.

My meaning of domestic violence was all wrong.

I watched videos, read articles and educated myself on something I wished I had learned years ago. I learned that domestic violence can occur in communities of all religious and ethnic backgrounds, all ages, any gender, any social class. I learned physical abuse is only one of the many forms of abuse that defined domestic violence. I learned that anyone could become a victim of domestic violence and there isn't a mold of a "perfect victim".

The National Hotline defines domestic violence as *a pattern of behaviors used by one partner to maintain power and control over another partner in an intimate relationship.* Now the red flags were playing back in my memory and the further back I went, the more signs I saw. *There is a fine line between loving someone and becoming obsessive and controlling.*

People have this strange idea that they are invincible. That horrific tragedies can happen around us but never could it happen to us. *Being a strong and independent woman does not mean we should be ashamed to reach out for help.* Sometimes an outside perspective from someone who has your best interests at heart is more clear than our own.

Jasmine never told me she feared him. I don't think she ever believed her life was in danger until her final moments. I always wonder if she called out for me or for anyone. Did neighbors hear her cries and dismiss them? Was she afraid?

Defensive wounds confirmed to us that she put up one hell of a fight. What was he thinking? What could make someone snap in the blink of an eye and shatter so many lives? Why do bad things happen to good people?

He robbed us of the moments we were supposed to have and all the plans that we made. He robbed the world of all the good Jasmine was going to do but I refuse to give him that power. Sometimes I still struggle with the idea that Jasmine is another victim of domestic violence. Sometimes I honestly believe that she met someone who was sick and because she had a good heart, she chose to stay with him. She knew leaving him would break his heart - she said that to me. Jasmine was selfless: she would sacrifice her happiness if she thought it would make someone else happy.

Do you believe in destiny?

That we are all put on earth with a purpose?

I knew Jasmine was going to do great things in life but I never considered the great things she could accomplish in death.

There is no shame in dying. What will your legacy be?

As much as it hurts me, I believe that helping others through Jasmine's story is my purpose. It is now my purpose to carry on my sister's legacy. I know she would have done it for me. Did Jasmine die so that other women could live? I don't know. What I do know is that her story has touched lives globally. I get messages every day that another woman has left her abuser. That a loved one has stepped in and interfered and helped someone get out, that someone has decided to learn more and judge less.

I would be doing Jasmine a huge disservice if I allowed the world to forget her.

After Jasmine gained her wings, I founded a nonprofit organization in her memory. The Jasmine Nunez Foundation strives to bring awareness to domestic violence through education. Our hope is that the awareness sparks conversation, research and will lead to prevention. The more we share, the more we teach. The more we teach, the more lives we save. Jasmine's story resonates with women because they see themselves in Jasmine. Jasmine could've been your sister, your best friend, your cousin, your classmate.

The Jasmine Nunez Foundation has organized events and marches in Massachusetts and New York since 2011. I became a certified domestic violence counselor in 2014. I have spent most of my time speaking at universities and community panels to share Jasmine's story and offer my support to those survivors. Television networks such as TV One and Investigation Discovery have shared Jasmine's story and allowed me the platform to reach a broader audience.

A plaque now hangs on the surgical technician floor at Mandl College commemorating Jasmine.

I was 20 years old when I lost my big sister. I had 20 years with her. I understand how lucky I am to have ever gotten the opportunity to have someone like her in my life, even though I wish we could've grown old together. I cannot deny the fact that I owe the woman I am today, to her. I have restored my faith and now I pray more, I love harder and I live unapologetically. I know my sister and I feel her around me always. She gives me that extra push on those days that I feel this battle is too big. I would give anything to have her here physically with me. I know none of the work I do will bring Jasmine back, but if I can stop even just one family from feeling the void my family feels every day without Jasmine, then I will continue to spread awareness and tell her story.

It has been years since I've seen my sister, since my mom has hugged her baby, and since my dad has kissed his little girl. It has been years that I've learned life's biggest lesson; *death does not discriminate. We are only here for a moment. This is borrowed time. Yes, we are only human and in this life we will experience troubles, heartaches and tragedies but when life knocks you down, redirect your energy. Find the beauty in the chaos, find the lesson in the sorrow and Dream BIG! Find your passion, whatever it is that makes you feel alive. Don't wait, do it now.* There is no excuse to waste your life. Someone else just took their last breath.

Sometimes I feel like Jasmine lives through me. I was terrified of flying; now I cannot stay off of a plane. All I want to do is experience the different landscapes, cultures and people of the world. That makes me feel alive. Helping others by sharing Jasmine's story makes me feel like she is alive. My sister is a beautiful soul and she will always be remembered by how she put others before herself. Her infectious laugh and radiant smile is something that I will never forget. I try to live every day of my life like tomorrow is the end because if it is, I want to be remembered like Jasmine Maxine Nunez; happy and full of life.

Signs you're in a toxic relationship

* Physical violence
* Feelings of exhaustion, emptiness or sadness after a conversation or interaction
* Not feeling like yourself
* Continuous criticism
* Lack of support (ideas, children, career)
* Controlling behavior (keeping you away from family and friends)
* Negative financial behaviors
* Patterns of disrespect (cheating, lying, feelings not being validated)
* Second-guessing yourself
* Self-esteem declining
* Ignoring your needs
* There's a clear imbalance of power
* Making excuses for your partner's bad behavior.
*Lack of self-care
*Scared to ask a question or ask for help
*Isolation

Tips on leaving a toxic relationship

Find support - a therapist, family member, and sympathetic friends

Become more autonomous - create a life for you. Begin to sign up for hobbies and other interests.

Build your self-esteem with affirmations, journaling, and reading. Reading will help you gain knowledge on toxic relationships versus healthy relationships.

Set Boundaries - your responsibility is you and your health. No one comes before You and What's Best For You.

Master the art of self-love, study it and master it

Seek shelter for a new place to live

Maintain strict no contact with the other person. Detach.

BREAK THE CYCLE

"And one day she discovered that she is fierce and strong, and full of fire and that not even she could hold herself back because her passion burned brighter than her fears."
-Mark Anthony

Artist GYPSY of Springfield, Massachusetts draws an image of a woman whose life was taken due to reckless violence.

I Got Flowers Today

I got flowers today!
It wasn't our anniversary or any other special day; last night he threw me into
a wall and then started choking me; it seemed unreal, a nightmare, but you
wake up from nightmares and I woke up this morning sore and bruised all
over - but I know he is sorry; because he sent me flowers today.
-Paulette Kelly

JANALIZ

"My Life is my message." - Mahatma Gandhi

"I'm going to be bald!" were the words replaying in my mind.

Everyone that I loved flashed right before my eyes. *The remembrance of their love gave me a sense of security. Death was the last thing on my mind.*

I was eighteen years old when I was diagnosed with Cancer (Hodgkin's Lymphoma).

I had no knowledge of what cancer was.

I did my own research and found out I had cancer before the

doctors diagnosed me. Every word the doctors mentioned to me that I didn't understand I quickly searched up. Google knows everything. I was just a regular teen who loved dancing, hanging out with friends and braiding hair. I never really thought I would be in this position but things began to change rapidly and I had so many questions.

Hodgkin's lymphoma is a cancer of the lymphatic system, which is part of your immune system. Cells in the lymphatic system grow abnormally and may spread beyond it. - Mayoclinic.org

Have you ever received news that made you question everything about yourself? Or instantly you become confused? How did you react to the news? And what did you do to help yourself feel better?

I was five years old when my traumatic experiences started to happen.

I couldn't help but to question life after them.

I remember my mom being the only parent present growing up. My dad wasn't around much until my older years. I always questioned why, but never got answers.

I had this little voice in my head that guided me through my experiences. It would get louder at times and sometimes I wouldn't hear it at all. As I grew older, the experiences continued. All the unanswered questions created confusion within me. I felt alone and scared. I couldn't help but to question "Why me?"

Have you ever felt unsafe as a child? Have you ever questioned *why me?* What were your experiences growing up? How did you deal with them?

I felt this more and more as I got older.

It wasn't until I started my cancer journey that things flipped upside down. My mom moved to another state and I was on my own.

I was living with my boyfriend and his family at the time. Our relationship was filled with love but got a little rocky and filled with confusion when I was diagnosed with cancer. It was a difficult time. His mother took care of me through it all. She faithfully took off work every week to take me to chemotherapy and to take me to any appointments I needed to go to. She was there through my bad times, my happy times and even my angry and confused times. She was the true definition of an earth angel.

Life changed for me unexpectedly.

My hair started falling out, and I felt sick for weeks at a time. I stayed in my room in the dark and barely interacted with anyone. I had no motivation at all. But when I got sick of being alone and depressed, I would go out dancing and dance the night away. Dancing took everything away from me.

The pain was gone and my mind was at ease. The feeling I had inside was magical; it was like dancing with the stars and the universe.

What do you do to ease the pain from your experiences to keep you in a state of peace? How do you manage your emotions from interfering?

I remember one day I went to the movies instead of going out to dance. I put on a cute hat and out the door I was. Once I got there I immediately took my hat off because I felt a little uncomfortable and as I removed it, I noticed a group of teenagers on the opposite side of the room. They were pointing at me laughing and one of them shouted, "Look at her bald head. It's like she has cancer."

My tears immediately started to fall down my face. I felt so angry, so I shouted back, "I do have cancer and so what!"

They stood in complete shock with their mouths wide open.

I ran out of the movie theater and didn't look back. I've always feared being judged and that's exactly what happened. With no choice but to fight this disease, I became afraid of everything after that experience.

My self-esteem hit rock bottom. Those were the days I didn't hear that little voice in my head.

I was surrounded by so many people but felt so alone. I felt misunderstood, angry and confused. I just couldn't understand "Why I had to be the one going through this."

I felt like the world was bullying me.

Have you ever experienced bullying in your life? How did that impact you? Are you still impacted?

Things changed from one day to the other.

I became pregnant during chemotherapy after being told that it's really difficult to get pregnant while taking this medication.

Here I am carrying a baby in my belly.

At this point I had gone through six rounds of chemo and was in remission.

I was so happy to be off treatment. I was so sure my cancer was gone. I felt really good internally.

A month later, my cancer relapsed and now it was at a stage 4 with a survival rate of 15%.

Doctors suggested starting a different type of chemotherapy that was more intense than the one I'd taken before. That meant being an inpatient at the hospital during this time and terminating my pregnancy.

In denial, I refused medication and continued my pregnancy.

Everyone around me was afraid for my life. They begged me to go on with the treatment.

I questioned their faith in me and why they were afraid and I wasn't.

With high spirits, I continued my pregnancy and four months in, everything hit me. I couldn't walk. I was so weak and for the first time during this journey I felt like I was actually dying. I didn't have the strength to get up at all. My body felt so drained and exhausted.

I remember trying to make myself a sandwich and literally dragging myself on the floor just to make it to the kitchen. The pain was unbearable. My life flashed before my eyes.

In tears, I held my belly and immediately called my doctors and continued with their plan.

I went through a painful termination of pregnancy that led me into a deep depression and grief period. Waking up from anesthesia I was instantly in tears. I felt the emptiness inside me. I felt like a piece of me was missing.

As I looked over to the table next to my bed, there was a blue box. I grabbed it and inside was a paper with little footprints and a message that said, *"When hello means Goodbye. My unborn is now my guardian angel and I am alive. A life for a Life."*

I couldn't help but to see life so differently after this.

Have you ever been through an experience that changed your views on life drastically? What happened that changed your perception? And how has it served you in the now moments?

I couldn't help but to be grateful for life. I continued chemotherapy and prepared for my transplant after two whole weeks of radiation. The days went by and the seasons changed.

I noticed I didn't question, "Why me" anymore.

I became stronger and felt stronger.

The little voice in my head was loud again and continued to guide me during this process.

I separated from my boyfriend and a year later found someone new.

It was an instant connection.

After three years of fighting cancer I was done. I BEAT CANCER TWICE!

It was the best moment of my life.

I was excited to see my friends and family. I enjoyed myself as much as I could being cancer free. That was the moment I wanted for life.

A few months passed and I started to feel really afraid, knowing I had to follow up on my cancer. I would shake and my heart would palpitate, almost knocking me out.

Every experience I've been through, every emotion I felt during these traumatic experiences would come right back up. It was hard for me to adapt to life after cancer. I developed PTSD, and Anxiety/Panic attacks. That stopped me from so many things I wanted to do.

Do you ever feel like the obstacles never stop? What makes you feel this way? What thoughts come up? How do you manage them?

ON JUNE 6, 2012, a year after my remission, life took a spin for the better.

I became a mother.

I REMEMBER like it was yesterday.

I walked all day this day, morning to the afternoon. I took the most peaceful nap I had taken my whole pregnancy. I felt so warm and light.

When I woke up I remember having a one on one with God. I expressed how badly I wanted my baby to be healthy and felt really uncomfortable and just wanted her to come out. I expressed my gratitude toward life and seconds later, my water broke.

I was in complete shock. I kind of chuckled a bit when it happened.

GOD answered my prayers.

I rushed to get my daughter's father and soon after headed to the hospital. My daughter was born at 12:20am. I was in love again for the first time. I felt like I could breathe and live again. My daughter gave me so much life just looking into her eyes. She motivated me in so many ways. She gave me the strength to keep going.

As she grew older, her father and I separated and I moved out of state with family and continued my passion of braiding and my career as a cosmetologist.

Have you ever felt like it was the end of the world for you and something just brings you back to life? What experience was it that changed you drastically? What did you notice that held you back? How did you keep that momentum?

BEING a single mother was a bit difficult for me to adjust to.

I never really saw my mom loved by a man. She never settled and when she tried, it seemed like she was by herself anyway. She worked and took care of everything. She did the best she could raising all six of her children. She had to learn to be a mother at a young age after her mom passed away in her earlier years growing up. I tried to understand as much as I could when it came to my parents. I know deep down the issues were deeper. Being a mother myself and dealing with certain issues in my life I became aware of this.

My mom is in a different place in her life now due to the things she endured throughout the years and if I can explain our relationship, it's a burst of love when we see each other. This took a lot of understanding and forgiveness. As I heal, those around me heal as well. I don't need a perfect mom, I just need a happy one.

I've learned a lot from just observing and that alone led me into my journey of self-healing. I started healing my inner child and discovered that a lot of what we think we are, is really not what we are. A lot of it was passed down through generations and destructive ways of living growing up. It was all programming.

I developed "codependency" through my childhood trauma. Feeling alone, unsafe, and the fear of being judged are all symptoms of that. All of my relationships were mirrors of everything I ever felt inside me.

Now, I have a better understanding why things were the way

they were. Knowing that I based my self-esteem around trying to make everyone happy was a big piece of my problem. I just wanted to fit in so I accepted a lot of behaviors and manipulation from others.

As a child, I felt like no one could hear me so I felt abandoned and rejected and that too created the need to always find attachment with everything, including people. I wanted to be seen and heard.

LOVE was all I needed and when you grow up feeling the way I did, you don't know when to love yourself because that's what you were taught. If your parents didn't give you love when you needed it then they taught you how to not love yourself.

Having that knowledge now and observing how everything in my life played out, I dedicated my life to self-love. That entailed me being my own parent. Digging inside of me and hugging that little girl that needed all the attention and love and giving it to her.

This was my breakthrough!

DO you have symptoms of codependency? Are you ready to heal from it?

That voice in my head that guided me through all my experiences, I've trusted it since I was five. That was my intuition. It led me to discover me. Your intuition gives you the ability to understand something immediately, without the need for conscious reasoning. My intuition led me to be the WOMAN THAT KNOWS HER WORTH AND NEEDS NO VALIDATION FROM THE EXTERNAL WORLD TO BE THE QUEEN THAT SHE IS. THE GODDESS SHE WAS BORN AS, AND THE NURTURING AND COMPASSIONATE MOTHER SHE IS HERE TO BE.

I remember when I used to ask, "Why me?"

Well, WHY NOT ME?

My Story Continues...

Have you started your self-love journey yet? What are you waiting for?

You deserve to be loved.

Self-Love Checklist

Check them off as you complete or write them into your daily agenda

* Use your words to build yourself up
    * Give yourself what you need when you need it
    * Live gratefully
    * Set boundaries
    * Learn to love your body
    * Write yourself a love letter
    * Slow down, be present and mindful
    * Unplug for a day from technology
    * Use daily affirmations
    * Dance to your favorite song
    * Practice self-compassion
    * Utilize the power of positive thinking
    * Embrace your imperfections
    * Let go of your anger
    * Take a self-defense class
    * Start eating healthier

Surround yourself with loving and supportive people
No negative self-talk
Acknowledge who you already are and what you have accomplished
Tell yourself your good qualities
Meditate
LEARN TO SAY NO

"The human spirit is stronger than anything that can happen to it." - C. C. Scott

A.J. The Artist of Springfield Massachusetts draws an image entitled "Fight", exposing what lies beneath.
She states:
"I fight to survive.
I fight to work.

I fight to become better than myself.
I fight to have the same opportunities that others have and more.
I fight to keep moving forward despite my struggles and shortcomings.
I'm fighting to stay alive in this world called life."

If I can make you see things from a different perspective
Will you accept it?
Or will you continue to be a closed chamber with locks that can't be opened
Or walls that can't be broken?
See life for me was a bit different
I've seen everything with different eyes that caused a lot of lies and beliefs
within me but I'm here to shift it
With the power inside of me that's been buried and burning inside of me
I am powerful, I am Great, I am me
Me - a spiritual being living a human experience. That's me. Will you
accept me?
No need to answer for which I have the answer
To every question I've ever asked and it wasn't til I healed my past
Trauma, inner child wounds and self-beliefs
That things seemed clearer.
-Janaliz Lebreault

Dear Mom,
I wish I knew you a little more
So I could understand you a little bit more
I can't imagine how it feels to lose your mom
I don't want to lose you mom
I use to be able to talk to you about everything
But now I can't
You have so many things running through your mind you can't
I get it...
I know how you feel
Sometimes it's hard to feel
But We are connected
I am a part of you
Just look at your reflection.
I don't want to lose you
See Grandma has been with you since
And still is
Those sleepless nights, when nothing seem right
She was there. And still is.
You can love again, and smile again
You deserve to
But it's up to you
Take a deep breath and just let go of everything that felt like the flu
If you don't believe in yourself then I do!
Despite every obstacle, you made it through, and she was there too!
Watching you go through the process made me progress. I am a mother
And I need my mother too.
I love you.
-Janaliz Lebreault

Sonia

"I am not a victim; I am a survivor."

My name is Sonia Quiles and as many people know me, I am Sonia from the *Educate with Sonia* show and today, I'll be telling you a short version of my story.

I was eighteen years old when I left Puerto Rico to live in the United States.

Regardless of my young age, I got on a plane with my six-month-old daughter with no money or winter clothes, no family, and I did not speak English.

If you only knew what I was running from maybe you would understand why I left. I truly wanted a better life for me and my daughter.

"The future belongs to those who give the next generation reason for hope."
-Pierre Teilhard de Chardin

Artist Frankie Borrero of New York City paints an image of his daughter emphasizing the beautiful features of his Latina child.

"Am I supposed to be alive? How much more can I take? When will this process end? Is this the cross that I need to carry?"

These are the questions that I asked God every day. I grew up with an alcoholic mother and she was absent more than present a lot of the time. We didn't celebrate holidays, graduations, or any special events and I quickly learned how to survive on my own.

Even though at a young age I learned how to be strong, I was not afraid of death. I wanted to die many times and tried to commit suicide three times.

But God had other plans for me.

At the age of fifteen, my mother became very ill and passed away from cirrhosis of the liver. While she was ill, I cared for her for eight months until she passed away. I was broken, but even in the darkness, I had an angel to guide me.

Luz Milagros was my older sister and she introduced me to God, which is the reason why I kept on trying to live. *Have you ever had someone in your life who practically saved you or inspired you to keep living?* A few years later I gave birth to my daughter. My daughter was six months old when we left to the states - just me and my baby. I decided to move to the United States to create a better life.

My first apartment was in Holyoke, MA and was financed by the welfare department.

I slept on a box spring on the floor, I had no curtains and I kept my food stored between my windows. *Have you ever had to start over and build from nothing? Have you felt as though it was either survive or die?*

My rent was $375 and I only received $395 in monthly bene-fits. Do the math. That left me with just $20 to take care of myself and my child. I did not have a GED and I did not have a high school education in Puerto Rico, so I was only receiving help for my daughter. I always wanted the best life that I could give her, so I decided to do better for myself and set a different example for her.

I started learning English at Holyoke Community College. It was a long process. I was trying to learn English, I was a new mom, and I was living in an entirely new place that was foreign. It was a lot at times but I didn't give up.

I took my GED in Spanish and I passed.

I continued at Holyoke Community College and worked hard to learn English. Next, I worked toward my associate degree. It has never been easy to speak clearly in another language and *it took me some time and some setbacks, but after 13 years, I finally got it.*

During the time I was working toward my degree, I met my now ex-husband. I gave birth to my second child, a son. From the day he was born, my son was really sick. During my pregnancy, I had chicken pox and that took a toll on him. He was very fragile and slept his first six months in a swing because he had chronic breathing problems.

During his first years, I took time off from school to focus on my growing family. During that time, my ex-husband started having hallucinations and was diagnosed with schizophrenia. I was being abused by him, I was financially insecure and I felt alone. *But again, I trusted God.* I was given the choice to either stay with him or leave with my children. For me, it wasn't a decision I had to think about. I left with my kids and never looked back.

Despite all I had gone through, I received my Associate Degree in Liberal Arts with a Certificate in Human Services. I began a career working in the human services field after graduating. *I had found a pace in my life that worked for me and my kids.*

In 2012, my ex-husband showed up to tear my life apart.

I fled the state of Massachusetts and moved to Connecticut. I had to leave my jobs and I had a hard time finding employment in Connecticut. *I knew that God said he would never forsake the people who loved him so I pressed on.* Since I had no luck finding a job, I applied to college and got a full scholarship to the University of

Hartford. It took me three years to finish my Bachelor's Degree in Psychology with a concentration in brain and behaviors and a minor in Management. At the same time, I was looking for a way to quickly make a lot of money the right way. I did some research and I became interested in real estate.

I graduated, got my real estate license and sold my first home, all in 2016. It was a year of major successes but also a year of major health issues. I was diagnosed with Fibromyalgia which still causes me pain today but I never let it defeat me.

Nevertheless, I have worked on myself in therapy for years addressing my traumas and I've challenged myself in other environments to grow with leaders from the community and even creating my own show, "Educate with Sonia".

The "Educate with Sonia" show brings resources to the community and my followers that helps them to become better citizens and leaders. I continue setting examples because even with the struggles, giving and helping is my calling and I know that lack of empathy is hurting our youth and our world. Giving back and being connected to the community is one of the things I want my children to learn and value. *What do you do to give back to others or to make a difference?*

If you are going through any struggle just remember, we don't stay stuck in time. Time cannot be recovered so choose wisely where and with whom you spend it. Be kind and live with integrity and help others because today you are here, but you never know where the crazy plane called life will take you tomorrow. Staying humble is the key to being resilient when we are faced with life's changes on this planet called Earth. We are all humans and believe it or not, we are all interconnected and we do need each other. Let's work together and love one another.

The biggest lessons for me in this journey of moving to the U.S. are that giving up in life should never be an option, facing the things that scare you the most are the things that will bring out the best in you, and that faith is crucial to continue thriving.

If you have faith you must also understand that what life holds for you comes by working diligently toward your vision. As much as I trust God, I know I have to make moves to see changes. This brings you growth but more importantly, wisdom.

Finally, understanding that you only can be accountable for your actions and being kind is never outdated. Love is the most powerful tool we have to do everything in life and a loving heart is absolutely necessary with the lack of leadership in our world today.

The Golden Rule says treat others the way you want to be treated, but I have my own version. Treat others better than the way you want to be treated. *Keep moving even if you stumble or fall; just get up and regroup, but never, never GIVE UP!*

God has a plan for you, so keep going!

A SOLDIER'S TIPS FOR SURVIVAL

1. LOVE YOURSELF EVERY SINGLE DAY
2. REMOVE NEGATIVE PEOPLE AND ALL THINGS THAT DO NOT SERVE YOU FROM YOUR LIFE
3. PRACTICE SELF-LOVE
4. ONLY INVEST IN ACTIVITIES THAT ARE BENEFICIAL TO YOU AND YOUR WELLBEING
5. TRUST YOUR INSTINCTS
6. TRY NEW THINGS
7. ALLOW YOURSELF TIME TO HEAL
8. DO WHATEVER IS NECESSARY TO HEAL
9. GO AFTER YOUR DREAM, ONE STEP AT A TIME.
10. MAKE A LIST OF ALL THE THINGS YOU LIKE ABOUT YOURSELF. READ THIS DAILY BEFORE BED

You kept your head above water
You knew that from the start
They would pull you directly under if you did not swim sweetheart
You fought off their viscous hands
Trying to drag you far below
You continued swinging through
The icy waters, ever slow
Though they clawed your body
Leaving marks upon your skin
You made it to the shore
While they drowned in all their sin.
-H.C.

You are not alone in your life's battles.
We Are Stronger Together."
-The Lady Soldiers

Artist Tiaunna Madison draws an image of a crowned woman draped in
words of power.
She states:
"With confidence you can find not only beauty and power within yourself; but

be strong enough to walk away from anyone or anything that doesn't contribute to your overall wellbeing."

Quotes
FOR OUR FELLOW SOLDIERS!

You have two options in life: stay a victim or become a survivor. It's your choice.
-Sonia Quiles

The most beautiful things on earth grow through DIRT… Keep glowing, keep flowing, keep growing.
-Janaliz Lebreault

Within each of us are the impressions of every experience we have had in our lifetime. The depth and texture of each one depends on our responses, our reactions during an experience.
- Jasmine Nunez (Melanie Nunez' late sister)

Turning your lessons into positivity and believing in yourself is when you truly start living.
-Regina Hudson

Sometimes the most beautiful things to ever happen to us arrive in unfamiliar and/or uncomfortable packages.
-Chaunacey Anne

"When your soul speaks, listen."
- Chaunacey Hill

"You are not alone. There is another woman somewhere in this world who has been or is in a similar situation. Be strong for yourself and for her."
-Regina Hudson

Affirmations

START YOUR DAY WITH ONE OR MORE AFFIRMATIONS

Stand in front of a mirror and say the statements provided. By doing this you release positivity into your life and brighten your mood and confidence. **Remember, your words are powerful.**

• *I love and accept myself for all that I am.*

• *I am worthy of health, wealth, and love.*

• *I inhale confidence and exhale fear.*

• *I am abundant in all areas of my life.*

• *What I want is already here or on its way.*

• *I release anything that does not serve me.*

• *I am at peace with my past.*

• I believe in me.

• I love the woman that I am.

• I am not my mistakes.

Every woman is a soldier. Every woman has a story
AND YOUR STORY MATTERS.
What battles have you overcome and where are you
headed? What have you learned from your losses and
victories? Tell Us Your Story.

THANK YOU TO OUR SPONSORS!

E.A.S.E. - Encouraging Another Sister's Excellence

The EASE organization exists to Encourage Another Sister's Excellence through supporting her personal, financial, relational, physical and spiritual evolution. We aim to uplift, educate and empower women to overcome and thrive in today's society, despite the challenges of life's experiences, cycles of hardship, negative circumstances and/or generational patterns.

Visit us on the web at easeinternational.org or give us a call or send a message at 470-888-1515.

After a personal journey riddled with its fair share of challenges, hardships, and negative circumstances, Aquana Raffington found a way to overcome and build a better life for herself and her family. With an affinity for numbers, a background in business management, and a great love of service to others, she turned her passion into profit as a life and financial coach. She later used that profit to fulfill her purpose of empowering other women to overcome their own hurdles and strive for their next level of excellence through the EASE Organization.

TLA CONSULTING

TLA Consulting consists of an advisory team of professionals that provide a wide range of solutions to a diverse client base including individuals, businesses, and organizations alike. We have years of experience in assisting and equipping clients with the solutions needed to sustain personal and professional growth and reach their full potential. We specialize in maximizing tax refunds, minimizing tax debt, restoring credit, proper business structure and formation, and home-buying coaching. Visit us on the web at consulttla.com or call 678-395-7818 now for your free 20-minute consultation. TLA Consulting, where problems meet solutions.

ARISE FOR SOCIAL JUSTICE

Arise for Social Justice with Executive Director Tanisha Arena, is a community organization dedicated to defending and advancing the rights of poor people. Arise has worked on issues such as housing, homelessness, criminal justice, environmental justice, and public health.

Their mission is to educate, organize, and unite low income people to know what their rights are, to stand up for those rights, to achieve those rights and to educate the community in social justice.

To learn more about Arise for Social Justice and support their mission, visit www.arisespringfield.org or call (413) 734-4948.

Tanisha Arena, M.S., Executive Director left the private sector for nonprofit to make a difference. "In the work I do, from being an author, a mentor for LGBTQ youth, a youth worker, domestic violence advocate and now Executive Director of Arise For Social Justice, my heart is in helping people identify and overcome barriers, figure out their best selves and then helping them get there.

I believe in connections, in the power of community, of telling our own stories and in speaking truth to power."

Shanndoll's boutique located in Springfield, MA has handmade jewelry, all natural organic sugar scrubs, flower baths, self-care kits, lip scrubs, body oils, and body jewelry. Shipping is available.

For more information call 203-802-1603 or visit @shanndollsboutique on Instagram and Shanndoll's Boutique on Facebook.

Kimmy is a fitness and health coach and is dedicated to making sure her clients get fit and healthy! She is a mother of two, a restaurant manager, and a fitness specialist.

If you are looking to get in shape, contact 413-335-5652 or Kcampbell63@yahoo.com or view https://kimberlycampbell.goherbalife.com/Catalog/Home/Index/en-US.

Kelly Laroe is an Executive Disability Advocate and consultant, also serves as an Educational Surrogate Parent for children in state custody. "I specialize in assisting preschool to post-secondary students transition with challenges such as ASD, trauma, specific learning disabilities, medical and behavioral issues. Because each child is unique in their learning style, it is necessary to ensure they are taught appropriately to achieve their learning potential.

When I'm not advocating for students, I spend time advocating for animals.

My inspiration comes directly from son Roderick. He has supported me and tolerated my schedule because he believes all children deserve a quality education.

I must thank Lady Soldiers for the honor of being a part of this brilliant and inspiring book. I stand with Lady Soldiers for talking about issues that are really hurting our communities."

Shirley Hudson-Givan

"Anything is possible, because anything you set your mind to you can do. I went through being married at the age of sixteen, getting divorced, becoming a single parent raising six boys, getting my degree, living through cancer, to be a 78 year old woman alive and well.
ANYTHING IS POSSIBLE."

Shirley Hudson Givan was a single mother of six boys and had her first child at the age of sixteen. Despite raising six children alone she still pursued her goals of going to college.
After ten years at American International College, Shirley had many important roles within her community. She worked as a day care voucher specialist, a career specialist, and as a supervisor of the Western Mass Day Care Facilities. Her favorite job of all was working for PAGE at the YWCA working with pregnant teenagers to help them obtain stability.
In 2002, Shirley was diagnosed with breast cancer, but because of her strength she beat breast cancer and is a Stage 3 survivor.

Meet The Authors

From left to right;
Janeliz Lebreault, Chaunacey A. Hill, Regina E. Hudson,
Melanie M. Nunez, Sonia Quiles

Author and Founder of Lady Soldiers, Regina Hudson, also the owner of Hudson Financial Strategies, identified a need for financial literacy and investing in education. She became licensed as a life insurance specialist and began conducting financial and homeownership seminars. She is dedicated to helping families become financially secure and knowledgeable. A life insurance specialist, event host, and women empowerment leader, Regina Hudson's mission is to inspire others to be the best versions of themselves.

Author Chaunacey Hill applied all her trades and pushed full force creating a one-stop-shop multi-craft business. Her mission in life is to promote creativity in everyone who will allow it. She wants women to know that there is always a choice and there is no need to attempt to fit into any mold society has projected onto them. She stands by her slogan, "Be Great, Create, Repeat!"

Author Melanie Nuñez founded the Jasmine Nunez Foundation to spread awareness and keep her sister's legacy alive. Among other things, Melanie is a certified domestic violence counselor and has organized awareness events throughout the northeast. Most recently, Melanie appeared on the TV shows *Web of Lies* and *Fatal Attraction,* which reached millions of viewers across the world!

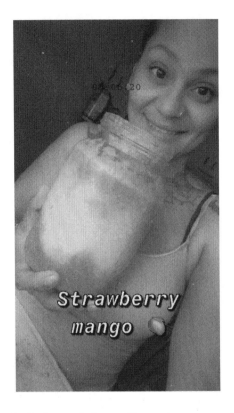

Author Janaliz Lebreault is a self-taught master-braider and natural juice creator. She is one with ALL and expresses her love for humanity through sharing her story. She dedicates her life to self-love and learning and growing internally so she can share her knowledge to everyone looking to connect back to love. She aspires to become a Self-Love Coach in the future to help guide others to have a healthy mind, healthy relationships, and overall healthy life.

Author and Sponsor Sonia Quiles is a real estate agent, community activist and host of her own show, Educate With Sonia, on the Digital BoomBox Network. Sonia has been a real estate agent for over six years and helps individuals and families find the right home for the right price. Her show, *Educate with Sonia*, features guests with information on navigating social systems and provides resources encouraging everyone to become engaged in their communities and utilize resources available.

Thank you for reading our book and we hope you appreciate our truth, stories, and advice. We Truly Are Stronger Together.

If you are interested in telling your story in the next volume of Lady Soldiers, contact us at theladysoldiers@gmail.com.

Also make sure to visit our website www.theladysoldiers.com and subscribe to stay involved with the Lady Soldiers Movement.

Made in the USA
Middletown, DE
30 October 2020